MW01102626

C. Casey

PASSWORD JOURNAL
LOGBOOK

Wingfeather Books

wingfeatherbooks.com

Cover art and interior design by Cheryl Casey
Copyright © 2015 Cheryl Casey

ISBN-13: 978-1522981947
ISBN-10: 1522981942

Name: ~~Ale~~ *Pink - Night*

Phone: *Blue morning*

Mobile:

Email:

Address:

A

Website:	
Login:	
Password:	**Date:**
Notes/Hints:	

Website:	
Login:	
Password:	**Date:**
Notes/Hints:	

A

Website:	
Login:	
Password:	Date:
Notes/Hints:	

Website:	
Login:	
Password:	Date:
Notes/Hints:	

A

Website:	
Login:	
Password:	Date:
Notes/Hints:	

Website:	
Login:	
Password:	Date:
Notes/Hints:	

A

Website:	
Login:	
Password:	Date:
Notes/Hints:	

Website:	
Login:	
Password:	Date:
Notes/Hints:	

B

Website:	
Login:	
Password:	**Date:**
Notes/Hints:	

Website:	
Login:	
Password:	**Date:**
Notes/Hints:	

B

Website:	
Login:	
Password:	Date:
Notes/Hints:	

Website:	
Login:	
Password:	Date:
Notes/Hints:	

B

Website:	
Login:	
Password:	Date:
Notes/Hints:	

Website:	
Login:	
Password:	Date:
Notes/Hints:	

B

Website:	
Login:	
Password:	Date:
Notes/Hints:	

Website:	
Login:	
Password:	Date:
Notes/Hints:	

B

Website:	
Login:	
Password:	Date:
Notes/Hints:	

Website:	
Login:	
Password:	Date:
Notes/Hints:	

B

Website:	
Login:	
Password:	Date:
Notes/Hints:	

Website:	
Login:	
Password:	Date:
Notes/Hints:	

C

Website:	
Login:	
Password:	Date:
Notes/Hints:	

Website:	
Login:	
Password:	Date:
Notes/Hints:	

C

Website:	
Login:	
Password:	Date:
Notes/Hints:	

Website:	
Login:	
Password:	Date:
Notes/Hints:	

C

Website:	
Login:	
Password:	**Date:**
Notes/Hints:	

Website:	
Login:	
Password:	**Date:**
Notes/Hints:	

C

Website:	
Login:	
Password:	Date:
Notes/Hints:	

Website:	
Login:	
Password:	Date:
Notes/Hints:	

C

Website:	
Login:	
Password:	Date:
Notes/Hints:	

Website:	
Login:	
Password:	Date:
Notes/Hints:	

C

Website:	
Login:	
Password:	Date:
Notes/Hints:	

Website:	
Login:	
Password:	Date:
Notes/Hints:	

D

Website:	
Login:	
Password:	**Date:**
Notes/Hints:	

Website:	
Login:	
Password:	**Date:**
Notes/Hints:	

D

Website:	
Login:	
Password:	Date:
Notes/Hints:	

Website:	
Login:	
Password:	Date:
Notes/Hints:	

D

Website:

Login:

Password:	Date:

Notes/Hints:

Website:

Login:

Password:	Date:

Notes/Hints:

D

Website:	
Login:	
Password:	**Date:**
Notes/Hints:	

Website:	
Login:	
Password:	**Date:**
Notes/Hints:	

D

Website:	
Login:	
Password:	Date:
Notes/Hints:	

Website:	
Login:	
Password:	Date:
Notes/Hints:	

D

Website:	
Login:	
Password:	Date:
Notes/Hints:	

Website:	
Login:	
Password:	Date:
Notes/Hints:	

E

Website:	
Login:	
Password:	Date:
Notes/Hints:	

Website:	
Login:	
Password:	Date:
Notes/Hints:	

Website:

Login:

Password:	Date:

Notes/Hints:

| |
| |

Website:

Login:

Password:	Date:

Notes/Hints:

| |
| |

E

Website:

Login:

Password:	Date:

Notes/Hints:

Website:

Login:

Password:	Date:

Notes/Hints:

Website:

Login:

Password:	Date:

Notes/Hints:

Website:

Login:

Password:	Date:

Notes/Hints:

E

Website:	
Login:	
Password:	Date:
Notes/Hints:	

Website:	
Login:	
Password:	Date:
Notes/Hints:	

E

Website:	
Login:	
Password:	**Date:**
Notes/Hints:	

Website:	
Login:	
Password:	**Date:**
Notes/Hints:	

F

Website:	
Login:	
Password:	Date:
Notes/Hints:	

Website:	
Login:	
Password:	Date:
Notes/Hints:	

F

Website:	
Login:	
Password:	Date:
Notes/Hints:	

Website:	
Login:	
Password:	Date:
Notes/Hints:	

F

Website:	
Login:	
Password:	Date:
Notes/Hints:	

Website:	
Login:	
Password:	Date:
Notes/Hints:	

Website:	
Login:	
Password:	Date:
Notes/Hints:	

Website:	
Login:	
Password:	Date:
Notes/Hints:	

F

Website:	
Login:	
Password:	Date:
Notes/Hints:	

Website:	
Login:	
Password:	Date:
Notes/Hints:	

Website:	
Login:	
Password:	Date:
Notes/Hints:	

Website:	
Login:	
Password:	Date:
Notes/Hints:	

G

Website:	
Login:	
Password:	Date:
Notes/Hints:	

Website:	
Login:	
Password:	Date:
Notes/Hints:	

G

Website:	
Login:	
Password:	Date:
Notes/Hints:	

Website:	
Login:	
Password:	Date:
Notes/Hints:	

G

Website:	
Login:	
Password:	Date:
Notes/Hints:	

Website:	
Login:	
Password:	Date:
Notes/Hints:	

G

Website:	
Login:	
Password:	**Date:**
Notes/Hints:	

Website:	
Login:	
Password:	**Date:**
Notes/Hints:	

G

Website:	
Login:	
Password:	Date:
Notes/Hints:	

Website:	
Login:	
Password:	Date:
Notes/Hints:	

G

Website:	
Login:	
Password:	Date:
Notes/Hints:	

Website:	
Login:	
Password:	Date:
Notes/Hints:	

Website:	
Login:	
Password:	Date:
Notes/Hints:	

Website:	
Login:	
Password:	Date:
Notes/Hints:	

H

Website:	
Login:	
Password:	**Date:**
Notes/Hints:	

Website:	
Login:	
Password:	**Date:**
Notes/Hints:	

H

Website:	
Login:	
Password:	Date:
Notes/Hints:	

Website:	
Login:	
Password:	Date:
Notes/Hints:	

Website:	
Login:	
Password:	Date:
Notes/Hints:	

Website:	
Login:	
Password:	Date:
Notes/Hints:	

H

Website:	
Login:	
Password:	**Date:**
Notes/Hints:	

Website:	
Login:	
Password:	**Date:**
Notes/Hints:	

Website:	
Login:	
Password:	Date:
Notes/Hints:	

Website:	
Login:	
Password:	Date:
Notes/Hints:	

Website:

Login:

Password:	**Date:**

Notes/Hints:

Website:

Login:

Password:	**Date:**

Notes/Hints:

I

Website:	
Login:	
Password:	Date:
Notes/Hints:	

Website:	
Login:	
Password:	Date:
Notes/Hints:	

I

Website:

Login:

Password: Date:

Notes/Hints:

Website:

Login:

Password: Date:

Notes/Hints:

Website:	
Login:	
Password:	Date:
Notes/Hints:	

Website:	
Login:	
Password:	Date:
Notes/Hints:	

Website:	
Login:	
Password:	Date:
Notes/Hints:	

Website:	
Login:	
Password:	Date:
Notes/Hints:	

I

Website:	
Login:	
Password:	**Date:**
Notes/Hints:	

Website:	
Login:	
Password:	**Date:**
Notes/Hints:	

J

Website:

Login:

Password:	**Date:**

Notes/Hints:

Website:

Login:

Password:	**Date:**

Notes/Hints:

J

Website:	
Login:	
Password:	**Date:**
Notes/Hints:	

Website:	
Login:	
Password:	**Date:**
Notes/Hints:	

J

Website:	
Login:	
Password:	Date:
Notes/Hints:	

Website:	
Login:	
Password:	Date:
Notes/Hints:	

J

Website:	
Login:	
Password:	Date:
Notes/Hints:	

Website:	
Login:	
Password:	Date:
Notes/Hints:	

J

Website:	
Login:	
Password:	Date:
Notes/Hints:	

Website:	
Login:	
Password:	Date:
Notes/Hints:	

J

Website:	
Login:	
Password:	Date:
Notes/Hints:	

Website:	
Login:	
Password:	Date:
Notes/Hints:	

Website:	
Login:	
Password:	**Date:**
Notes/Hints:	

Website:	
Login:	
Password:	**Date:**
Notes/Hints:	

Website:

Login:

Password:	Date:

Notes/Hints:

Website:

Login:

Password:	Date:

Notes/Hints:

K

Website:	
Login:	
Password:	Date:
Notes/Hints:	

Website:	
Login:	
Password:	Date:
Notes/Hints:	

K

Website:	
Login:	
Password:	Date:
Notes/Hints:	

Website:	
Login:	
Password:	Date:
Notes/Hints:	

Website:

Login:

Password: **Date:**

Notes/Hints:

Website:

Login:

Password: **Date:**

Notes/Hints:

K

Website:	
Login:	
Password:	Date:
Notes/Hints:	

Website:	
Login:	
Password:	Date:
Notes/Hints:	

L

Website:	
Login:	
Password:	Date:
Notes/Hints:	

Website:	
Login:	
Password:	Date:
Notes/Hints:	

L

Website:	
Login:	
Password:	Date:
Notes/Hints:	

Website:	
Login:	
Password:	Date:
Notes/Hints:	

L

Website:	
Login:	
Password:	Date:
Notes/Hints:	

Website:	
Login:	
Password:	Date:
Notes/Hints:	

L

Website:	
Login:	
Password:	Date:
Notes/Hints:	

Website:	
Login:	
Password:	Date:
Notes/Hints:	

L

Website:	
Login:	
Password:	Date:
Notes/Hints:	

Website:	
Login:	
Password:	Date:
Notes/Hints:	

L

Website:	
Login:	
Password:	Date:
Notes/Hints:	

Website:	
Login:	
Password:	Date:
Notes/Hints:	

Website:	
Login:	
Password:	**Date:**
Notes/Hints:	

Website:	
Login:	
Password:	**Date:**
Notes/Hints:	

M

Website:	
Login:	
Password:	**Date:**
Notes/Hints:	

Website:	
Login:	
Password:	**Date:**
Notes/Hints:	

Website:

Login:

Password: | **Date:**

Notes/Hints:

Website:

Login:

Password: | **Date:**

Notes/Hints:

M

Website:	
Login:	
Password:	Date:
Notes/Hints:	

Website:	
Login:	
Password:	Date:
Notes/Hints:	

Website:	
Login:	
Password:	Date:
Notes/Hints:	

Website:	
Login:	
Password:	Date:
Notes/Hints:	

Website:

Login:

Password:	**Date:**

Notes/Hints:

Website:

Login:

Password:	**Date:**

Notes/Hints:

N

Website:	
Login:	
Password:	Date:
Notes/Hints:	

Website:	
Login:	
Password:	Date:
Notes/Hints:	

Website:	
Login:	
Password:	Date:
Notes/Hints:	

Website:	
Login:	
Password:	Date:
Notes/Hints:	

N

Website:	
Login:	
Password:	Date:
Notes/Hints:	

Website:	
Login:	
Password:	Date:
Notes/Hints:	

Website:	
Login:	
Password:	Date:
Notes/Hints:	

Website:	
Login:	
Password:	Date:
Notes/Hints:	

N

Website:	
Login:	
Password:	Date:
Notes/Hints:	

Website:	
Login:	
Password:	Date:
Notes/Hints:	

Website:	
Login:	
Password:	Date:
Notes/Hints:	

Website:	
Login:	
Password:	Date:
Notes/Hints:	

O

Website:	
Login:	
Password:	Date:
Notes/Hints:	

Website:	
Login:	
Password:	Date:
Notes/Hints:	

O

Website:	
Login:	
Password:	Date:
Notes/Hints:	

Website:	
Login:	
Password:	Date:
Notes/Hints:	

O

Website:	
Login:	
Password:	Date:
Notes/Hints:	

Website:	
Login:	
Password:	Date:
Notes/Hints:	

O

Website:	
Login:	
Password:	Date:
Notes/Hints:	

Website:	
Login:	
Password:	Date:
Notes/Hints:	

O

Website:	
Login:	
Password:	Date:
Notes/Hints:	

Website:	
Login:	
Password:	Date:
Notes/Hints:	

Website:

Login:

Password:	**Date:**

Notes/Hints:

Website:

Login:

Password:	**Date:**

Notes/Hints:

P

Website:	
Login:	
Password:	Date:
Notes/Hints:	

Website:	
Login:	
Password:	Date:
Notes/Hints:	

Website:	
Login:	
Password:	**Date:**
Notes/Hints:	

Website:	
Login:	
Password:	**Date:**
Notes/Hints:	

P

Website:	
Login:	
Password:	Date:
Notes/Hints:	

Website:	
Login:	
Password:	Date:
Notes/Hints:	

Website:

Login:

Password:	**Date:**

Notes/Hints:

Website:

Login:

Password:	**Date:**

Notes/Hints:

P

Website:	
Login:	
Password:	**Date:**
Notes/Hints:	

Website:	
Login:	
Password:	**Date:**
Notes/Hints:	

Website:

Login:

Password:	**Date:**

Notes/Hints:

Website:

Login:

Password:	**Date:**

Notes/Hints:

Q

Website:	
Login:	
Password:	**Date:**
Notes/Hints:	

Website:	
Login:	
Password:	**Date:**
Notes/Hints:	

Q

Website:	
Login:	
Password:	**Date:**
Notes/Hints:	

Website:	
Login:	
Password:	**Date:**
Notes/Hints:	

Q

Website:

Login:

Password:	Date:

Notes/Hints:

Website:

Login:

Password:	Date:

Notes/Hints:

Website:	
Login:	
Password:	**Date:**
Notes/Hints:	

Website:	
Login:	
Password:	**Date:**
Notes/Hints:	

Q

Website:	
Login:	
Password:	Date:
Notes/Hints:	

Website:	
Login:	
Password:	Date:
Notes/Hints:	

Q

Website:	
Login:	
Password:	**Date:**
Notes/Hints:	

Website:	
Login:	
Password:	**Date:**
Notes/Hints:	

Website:

Login:

Password:	Date:

Notes/Hints:

| |
| |

Website:

Login:

Password:	Date:

Notes/Hints:

| |
| |

Website:	
Login:	
Password:	Date:
Notes/Hints:	

Website:	
Login:	
Password:	Date:
Notes/Hints:	

R

Website:	
Login:	
Password:	Date:
Notes/Hints:	

Website:	
Login:	
Password:	Date:
Notes/Hints:	

Website:

Login:

Password:	**Date:**

Notes/Hints:

Website:

Login:

Password:	**Date:**

Notes/Hints:

R

Website:	
Login:	
Password:	Date:
Notes/Hints:	

Website:	
Login:	
Password:	Date:
Notes/Hints:	

Website:

Login:

Password:	**Date:**

Notes/Hints:

Website:

Login:

Password:	**Date:**

Notes/Hints:

Website:

Login:

Password:	**Date:**

Notes/Hints:

Website:

Login:

Password:	**Date:**

Notes/Hints:

S

Website:	
Login:	
Password:	Date:
Notes/Hints:	

Website:	
Login:	
Password:	Date:
Notes/Hints:	

S

Website:	
Login:	
Password:	**Date:**
Notes/Hints:	

Website:	
Login:	
Password:	**Date:**
Notes/Hints:	

S

Website:	
Login:	
Password:	Date:
Notes/Hints:	

Website:	
Login:	
Password:	Date:
Notes/Hints:	

S

Website:

Login:

Password:	Date:

Notes/Hints:

Website:

Login:

Password:	Date:

Notes/Hints:

S

Website:	
Login:	
Password:	Date:
Notes/Hints:	

Website:	
Login:	
Password:	Date:
Notes/Hints:	

T

Website:	
Login:	
Password:	Date:
Notes/Hints:	

Website:	
Login:	
Password:	Date:
Notes/Hints:	

Website:

Login:

Password:	**Date:**

Notes/Hints:

Website:

Login:

Password:	**Date:**

Notes/Hints:

T

Website:

Login:

Password:	**Date:**

Notes/Hints:

Website:

Login:

Password:	**Date:**

Notes/Hints:

T

Website:	
Login:	
Password:	Date:
Notes/Hints:	

Website:	
Login:	
Password:	Date:
Notes/Hints:	

T

Website:	
Login:	
Password:	Date:
Notes/Hints:	

Website:	
Login:	
Password:	Date:
Notes/Hints:	

Website:	
Login:	
Password:	**Date:**
Notes/Hints:	

Website:	
Login:	
Password:	**Date:**
Notes/Hints:	

U

Website:	
Login:	
Password:	**Date:**
Notes/Hints:	

Website:	
Login:	
Password:	**Date:**
Notes/Hints:	

U

Website:

Login:

Password:	**Date:**

Notes/Hints:

Website:

Login:

Password:	**Date:**

Notes/Hints:

Website:

Login:

Password:	Date:

Notes/Hints:

| |
| |

Website:

Login:

Password:	Date:

Notes/Hints:

| |
| |

U

Website:	
Login:	
Password:	Date:
Notes/Hints:	

Website:	
Login:	
Password:	Date:
Notes/Hints:	

Website:	
Login:	
Password:	Date:
Notes/Hints:	

Website:	
Login:	
Password:	Date:
Notes/Hints:	

Website:

Login:

Password:	Date:

Notes/Hints:

Website:

Login:

Password:	Date:

Notes/Hints:

Website:	
Login:	
Password:	Date:
Notes/Hints:	

Website:	
Login:	
Password:	Date:
Notes/Hints:	

Website:	
Login:	
Password:	**Date:**
Notes/Hints:	

Website:	
Login:	
Password:	**Date:**
Notes/Hints:	

Website:	
Login:	
Password:	Date:
Notes/Hints:	

Website:	
Login:	
Password:	Date:
Notes/Hints:	

Website:	
Login:	
Password:	Date:
Notes/Hints:	

Website:	
Login:	
Password:	Date:
Notes/Hints:	

Website:	
Login:	
Password:	Date:
Notes/Hints:	

Website:	
Login:	
Password:	Date:
Notes/Hints:	

Website:

Login:

Password:	**Date:**

Notes/Hints:

| |
| |

Website:

Login:

Password:	**Date:**

Notes/Hints:

| |
| |

Website:

Login:

Password: | **Date:**

Notes/Hints:

Website:

Login:

Password: | **Date:**

Notes/Hints:

Website:

Login:

Password:	Date:

Notes/Hints:

Website:

Login:

Password:	Date:

Notes/Hints:

X

Website:	
Login:	
Password:	**Date:**

Notes/Hints:

Website:	
Login:	
Password:	**Date:**

Notes/Hints:

Website:	
Login:	
Password:	Date:
Notes/Hints:	

Website:	
Login:	
Password:	Date:
Notes/Hints:	

Website:

Login:

Password:	**Date:**

Notes/Hints:

Website:

Login:

Password:	**Date:**

Notes/Hints:

Website:

Login:

Password:	**Date:**

Notes/Hints:

Website:

Login:

Password:	**Date:**

Notes/Hints:

Y

Website:	
Login:	
Password:	Date:
Notes/Hints:	

Website:	
Login:	
Password:	Date:
Notes/Hints:	

Y

Website:	
Login:	
Password:	**Date:**
Notes/Hints:	

Website:	
Login:	
Password:	**Date:**
Notes/Hints:	

Y

Website:	
Login:	
Password:	Date:
Notes/Hints:	

Website:	
Login:	
Password:	Date:
Notes/Hints:	

Website:

Login:

Password:	Date:

Notes/Hints:

Website:

Login:

Password:	Date:

Notes/Hints:

Z

Website:	
Login:	
Password:	**Date:**
Notes/Hints:	

Website:	
Login:	
Password:	**Date:**
Notes/Hints:	

Website:

Login:

Password:	**Date:**

Notes/Hints:

Website:

Login:

Password:	**Date:**

Notes/Hints:

Z

Website:

Login:

Password: Date:

Notes/Hints:

Website:

Login:

Password: Date:

Notes/Hints:

Z

Website:	
Login:	
Password:	Date:
Notes/Hints:	

Website:	
Login:	
Password:	Date:
Notes/Hints:	

Made in the USA
Middletown, DE
09 January 2019